First published 2010 by Kingfisher
This edition published 2023 by Kingfisher
an imprint of Macmillan Children's Books
The Smithson, 6 Briset Street, London, EC1M 5NR
Associated companies throughout the world
www.panmacmillan.com

EU representative: Macmillan Publishers Ireland Ltd, 1st Floor,
The Liffey Trust Centre, 117-126 Sheriff Street Upper, Dublin 1, D01 YC43

Consultants: Alison Boyle, Curator, Astronomy and Modern Physics, the
Science Museum, London; and with additional thanks to Jonathan Chase.

ISBN 978-0-7534-4887-8

Copyright © Macmillan Children's Books 2010, 2023

Illustrations © Nishant Choksi 2010, 2023
www.nishantchoksi.com

All rights reserved. No part of this publication may be reproduced, stored
in or introduced into a retrieval system or transmitted in any form or by
any means (electronic, mechanical, photocopying, recording or otherwise),
without the prior written permission of the publisher. Any person who
does any unauthorised act in relation to this publication may be
liable to criminal prosecution and civil claims for damages.

1 3 5 7 9 8 6 4 2
1TR/0423/UTD/WKT/140MA

A CIP catalogue record for this book is available from the British Library.

Printed in China

This book is sold subject to the condition that it shall not, by way of trade or otherwise,
be lent, resold, hired out, or otherwise circulated without the publisher's prior consent in
any form of binding or cover other than that in which it is published and without a similar
condition including this condition being imposed on the subsequent purchaser.

Note to readers: the website addresses listed in this book are correct at the time of going
to print. However, due to the ever-changing nature of the internet, website addresses
and content can change. Websites can contain links that are unsuitable for children.
The publisher cannot be held responsible for changes in website addresses or
content, or for information obtained through third-party websites. We strongly
advise that internet searches should be supervised by an adult.

REALLY BIG Questions FOR DARING THINKERS

SPACE AND TIME

Mark Brake

Illustrated by
Nishant Choksi

CONTENTS

6 Introduction: What on Earth is going on up there?

CHAPTER 1
RECIPE FOR A UNIVERSE

10 Why do we think there was a beginning to the Universe at all?
11 Was everything cooked up in one go?
11 When did the Universe start?
12 How on Earth can we describe the Universe from here?
14 How did we explain the Universe before science came along?
16 Does the Universe follow a recipe?
17 How do we measure the Universe?
17 Is there a map of the Universe?
18 What is the Universe made of?
19 Why is the night sky so dark?
19 What shape is the Universe?
20 Is space smelly?
21 Is the Universe getting bigger?

CHAPTER 2
GOODNESS GRACIOUS, GREAT BALLS OF GAS!

24 How can the Sun be a dwarf?
26 What makes sunshine?
27 Do stars make noise?
28 Do stars live for ever?
29 Do stars explode?
29 Why do superstars live fast and die young?
30 Is anywhere completely dark?
31 Do black holes turn you into spaghetti?
31 What's at the centre of the Milky Way?
32 When stars die, what happens to all their stuff?
35 What's the difference between me, a planet, and a star?
36 What is light?
37 How quick is light?
37 Is what I'm seeing actually there?

CHAPTER 3
TIME, TIME AND TIME AGAIN

- 40 How did we put time together?
- 41 How do we know the age of things in space?
- 42 If a wardrobe has 3 dimensions, what is the 4th?
- 43 Does time always go at the same speed?
- 44 How is my body like a clock?
- 45 Is time the same on bigger planets?
- 46 How do you build a time machine?
- 47 Are there holes in space-time?

CHAPTER 4
THE GREAT BIG FUTURISTIC SPACE ADVENTURE

- 50 Where did science fiction begin?
- 51 Who invented space travel?
- 52 Was Neil Armstrong a modern explorer?
- 53 Who owns space?
- 54 Are there aliens in our solar system?
- 54 Are there other Earths?
- 55 Do aliens look like me?
- 56 If space is full of aliens, how come they haven't visited us yet?
- 57 Would aliens want to steal our stuff?

- 58 Glossary
- 62 Index
- 64 Further reading and how to think like a boffin

INTRODUCTION

WHAT ON EARTH IS GOING ON
UP THERE?
MARK BRAKE

Maybe tomorrow, or maybe a decade or a century from now, boffins may make the most shattering discovery of all time: evidence of alien life. What kind of space and time would these aliens inhabit? Where would they call home?

This book contains many questions such as these – questions that will stretch your brain and make you think.

Have you ever looked up and wondered, "Is there a map of the Universe?" or "Why is the night sky so dark?" While waiting for a bus have you asked yourself, "Does time always go at the same speed?" Or have you wished you lived on another planet and pondered, "Do aliens look like me?" All of these questions are asked in these pages, and many more besides.

Before you read these questions and the answers I've given, let's make one thing clear. While many of these questions have answers, many of them do not. Or they might have answers that will *change* in the future.

These questions are all 'scientific'. Science is what we call 'cumulative'. It sort of rewrites itself as new things are discovered and new ideas are formulated. Our ideas about things change as time goes by, so at any one time science can only really be thought of as:

"THE BEST CURRENT INTERPRETATION OF THE NATURAL WORLD"

You and I are designed for the purpose of living on Earth, which is a planet – a part of the cosmos, the Universe. But you and I are also *a part* of the Universe. We are made of the same materials that can be found on the other side of the Universe. Those materials may not be assembled in the same order, but they are basically the same.

So we can try to understand the Universe from this point of view, from the planet Earth, and build ideas about what things might be like 'out there'. But we can't touch, taste, see, hear and *feel* everything in the Universe close-up. At least, not yet.

Once you've read these pages you'll be tempted to think, "Is that it, then? Have we finally grasped what the Universe is like?" But the answer to that is: probably not. In fact, to even *suggest* that we understand the Universe is very *un*scientific. Science is all about questioning things – *all the time*. Even when we think our ideas are correct.

Who's to say people won't look back and laugh at our ideas about the Universe one day? So the golden rule is: *don't just listen to me – the Universe is right there in front of you... Take a good look for yourself.*

1

RECIPE FOR A UNIVERSE

BANG! And so the Universe began.

Many reckon that a huge *explosion* of space and time, known as the Big Bang, created the Universe. But the Universe as we know it is not fixed – it is *changing* all the time. It is changing right now, while you are reading these words.

And few things are changing faster, it seems, than our understanding of it. The more we learn, and the more questions we ask, the more the secrets of the cosmos seem to slip through our mortal fingers...

But that's no reason to give up. Let's keep on asking those tricky questions.

WHY
DO WE THINK THERE WAS A
BEGINNING
TO THE UNIVERSE AT ALL?

WAS EVERYTHING

From Earth, there are approximately 5,000 stars that you can see with the naked eye, and here and there you can make out the odd, hazy smudge of a galaxy. A galaxy is a huge swarm of stars, very far away in deep space, made up of billions upon billions of stars.

When astronomers observe the light from these galaxies, they find that the light is more 'red' than it should be. When this happens to light it's known as 'red shift', and it means that the galaxies are moving away from us.

Now, it's not just one or two galaxies that have this 'red-shifted' light... it's all of them! Billions of them, in fact!

If all the galaxies are moving away from one another today, that means that at some point in the distant past they were all in the same place...

That's why we think there was a 'beginning' to the Universe.

COOKED UP IN ONE GO?

Those big, bright balls of light we call stars are in many ways the building blocks of our Universe.

Stars are made mostly of hydrogen, which they burn for millions and billions of years. So, most of the Universe we see is made up of mega amounts of hydrogen. About 74 per cent of it, in fact. Almost 24 per cent of the Universe is helium, so that leaves just 2 per cent for everything else that exists...

All this hydrogen and helium was cooked up right at the beginning of the Universe, or so we think. The Universe likes to keep things simple, and hydrogen and helium are as simple as it gets for stuff. Everything else was cooked up *inside* the stars, for many generations after the beginning of the Universe.

That means that almost everything else you see on Earth is made of what we might call the *heavy stuff*. Yes, the carbon in your skin, the iron in your blood, and the gold in the World Cup – these were all cooked up by stars over the course of history.

WHEN DID THE UNIVERSE START?

Nothing ever happens 'immediately'. This is because light takes time to reach the human eye (even though it is travelling at a speedy 300,000 kilometres per second). So, as you watch your cat getting its head trapped in the fridge door, that actually happened the tiniest fraction of a second ago.

So, in a way, your cat is time travelling.

For this reason, we can think of stargazing as a form of time travel.

Our Universe is so unimaginably vast that from its outer limits, light takes longer than twice the age of the Earth to reach our telescopes. And because it takes so much time for light to travel across these vast distances in space, everything in the Universe has a *look-back time*.

The further out we look, the further back in time we are gazing. And since the look-back time for those outer reaches of the Universe is around 13.75 billion years, we use that measurement to mark the very beginning of time.

HOW **ON EARTH** CAN WE DESCRIBE THE UNIVERSE FROM **HERE?**

The simple answer is: by stargazing.

Humans have always looked upwards. In ancient times people used to judge the seasons, and the rotation of crops for food, based on the movements of the sky. And for centuries, people used the stars to navigate their ships.

Stargazing was an important part of life. And it still is.

When we watch the night sky, everything seems to revolve around the Earth. By night – stars, planets and galaxies rise in the east, then set in the west. By day – the Sun rises in the east, and sets in the west. So it's easy to get the idea that we are at the centre of everything!

Aha! But then we found out it's just an illusion, down to the fact that the Earth turns around on its axis as it travels around the Sun.

Astronomy – the scientific study of the Universe – has taught us that the Earth is not at the centre of the Universe. Nor is it likely to be the only object of its kind, or made of materials only to be found on Earth. Not even the Sun is that special. The Sun is not at the centre of the Universe, nor is it the only star with planets around it, and now we know that it will not keep burning away in the sky for ever.

So, how about the Milky Way, our galaxy? No! That's not at the centre either. It's just one of 100 billion other galaxies, all adrift in an ever-expanding Universe, which we have discovered using our telescopes. Heck! There may even be other universes. Who's to say this is the only one?

It's amazing, when you think about it, that all these discoveries have been made from this one point in space – planet Earth – which is an extremely tiny ingredient in the grand recipe of everything.

HOW DID WE EXPLAIN THE UNIVERSE

We all love a good story. Stories shape what we see, what we do, and what we dream. But stories are also how we make sense of the world. For thousands of years, since the beginning of early societies, people from different cultures have told their tales of the beginning of life, the Universe and everything. A lot of the time, these tales involve gods having fun or causing mischief.

In one story, which comes from West African culture, a giant sky-serpent-god moves his 7,000 coils, which form not just the hills and valleys of Earth, but also the stars and planets of the Universe. When he sheds his skin in the Sun, it releases all the waters over the Earth. Then the reflection of the Sun in the water creates the rainbow.

Lovely!

Another tale of creation, told by the native North American Kiowa Apache people, sounds like the world began with soccer. The story begins with darkness. Suddenly, from out of the darkness comes a thin disc – one side yellow, the other side white – and the disc hangs in mid-air. A small, bearded man then emerges and soon a tiny brown ball – not much larger than a bean – is kicked about by the gods until the ball expands to the size of the Earth...

BEFORE SCIENCE CAME ALONG?

In the modern, scientific age our understanding of the Universe has become much more practical. Nowadays we tend to create 'reasonable' stories about our Universe and how it might have come into being. Stories that can be tested by checking the facts as much as possible. Stories that make logical sense.

These days, people like to *see* what they believe. At least, *most* of the time.

Sure, it's still okay if you want to believe in any of the creation stories that have emerged from religions or popular mythology over the centuries. Who knows – any one of these theories of creation might be correct! Like I said right at the beginning, *don't take my word for it*.

BRAIN BURN!

The ancient Greeks named the Universe after their word for 'harmony' (*kosmos*). Do you think they chose the right word?

DOES THE UNIVERSE FOLLOW A RECIPE?

Imagine you wanted to take a chunk of Universe, like grabbing a handful of soil from the ground. And imagine you wanted that chunk to be just like any other chunk of Universe. In other words, you wanted it to be a 'typical' chunk, so that you could use it to make a repeatable 'Universe pattern'.

To do this, let us imagine the most gigantic ice-cream scoop of all time.

Using the scoop, we're going to scoop up that 'average' chunk of Universe. How big is it going to be, this chunk? It can't be solar-system sized, because our solar system is probably not the same as others. And it can't be galaxy sized, because our galaxy is just not the same as other galaxies.

Astronomers have worked out that the typical chunk you'd need to scoop, to get all this 'average stuff' in the Universe, is about 300 million light years across! Only then could we say that we had spotted a truly typical chunk of what the Universe is 'like' in other, distant parts of it.

HOW DO WE MEASURE THE UNIVERSE?

Light is the fastest thing known to science, but it still takes time for light to cover the vast distances across the Universe, from one object to another. So – as we've already said – we see things in space as they were in the past. The further we look out into space, the further we look back in time.

So using *time* is actually quite a sensible way to measure distances in space...

The journey of light from the Moon to the Earth takes around one second. We see the Moon as it looked a second ago, so the Moon is one 'light second' away. We see the Sun as it looked about eight minutes ago, so it's eight 'light minutes' from Earth.

Other stars are much further away. Even the next nearest star to Earth, Proxima Centauri, is about 40 million million (or 40 trillion) kilometres away. Light takes more than four years to travel from that nearby star and hit the naked eye. So it is four 'light years' away. We are looking at a four-year-old image of the star.

IS THERE A MAP OF THE UNIVERSE?

Maps of space are very tricky to make because all the stuff in the Universe is constantly on the move and the distances involved are huge. In deep space, unlike on Earth, you can't go visiting places to draw maps in detail. You have to make guesses by reading and measuring the starlight that comes to Earth.

The largest and most up-to-date maps of space are called red shift surveys. These are the biggest maps of the Universe that we can get. They show that galaxies are formed into immense clusters, separated by enormous voids of nothing. That's why astronomers call the large-scale map of the Universe a 'cosmic web'.

WHAT IS THE UNIVERSE MADE OF?

The Universe is basically made of two types of stuff. Stuff you can see, and stuff you can't.

We know a fair bit about the stuff you can see. It's what makes up planets, moons, stars and galaxies. All these things either give off light, or reflect it. Stars shine, and planets and moons reflect starlight. And galaxies are made up of millions upon millions of stars, so they shine too.

But recently, astronomers discovered that a sizeable portion of the Universe is missing.

It seems that all the 'light matter' (planets, moons, stars and galaxies) is just the tip of the cosmic iceberg. Scientists reckon that a lot of the *rest* of the Universe is made of some exotic, mysterious material known as 'dark matter' and a baffling phenomenon called 'dark energy'.

Dark matter is the stuff we *cannot* see. It is, if you like, the shadow of the Universe.

WHY IS THE NIGHT SKY SO DARK?

It is blue by day and dark at night. How come the sky is so *moody*?!

Sunlight is multi-coloured, and the air scatters blue light more than red, so the sky is mainly a cool blue colour during daytime. By evening, with the Sun lower in the sky, blue light is scattered out completely, so sunsets (and sunrises, too, for that matter) are often a warmer red colour.

But why is the night sky dark?

Okay, the Sun is facing the other side of the planet, so we're not receiving its light. But the Universe contains simply billions of stars, in all directions. So why isn't the sky a dazzling *white* at night?

There are two parts to the answer. Firstly, the light from stars and galaxies is travelling to us from all sorts of different distances across the Universe, so it does not reach us at the same time. Secondly, these objects are all of different ages, so the older ones will be dimming while the newer ones are shining brightly.

With me so far?

The result: at all times there is light from very distant objects that hasn't reached us yet and light from nearer objects, which is either dimming or shining brightly depending on the age of the stars and galaxies.

That, in a nutshell, is why the night sky is never filled with light.

WHAT SHAPE IS THE UNIVERSE?

Everyone's heard of Albert Einstein, right? He's the guy with the wild, white hair who rewrote the rules of science, early last century.

One of Uncle Albert's big ideas was this: mass bends space. Yes, that's right! The mass (amount of 'stuff') of something in space actually bends the space around it. And the more mass you have in one spot, the more curved that 'space spot' becomes.

Einstein also got to this big question: if space can be *bent*, by mass, then how might this affect the overall shape of the Universe?

In other words... If you think about this space-bending business on a larger scale, could the overall mass of all the stuff in the Universe give it a *curvy* shape?

We may never know for sure. But space boffins do think there are THREE possible Universe shapes: flat, spherical (ball-shaped) or hyperbolic (saddle-shaped).

IS SPACE SMELLY?

That very much depends on where you stick your nose.

Astronomers scouring the heart of our Milky Way Galaxy recently found that huge clouds of stuff are floating around there – the kind of stuff from which life on Earth is partly made. Not only that, but they think this stuff would taste a bit like raspberries... and smell like rum.

It's a big find, because it means that planets being formed at the galaxy's heart will already have some of the stuff vital for the development of life.

Other scientists, working at NASA, have also been banging their brains about pongs in space. When they interviewed astronauts about what space smells like, they were told different things by different space people. Some said space smelled of fried steak. Others spoke of hot metal. And others even said it reeked of welding a motorbike.

After all this, it's a bit of a disappointment to find out that this delicious space meal of hot metal soup (to start), fried steak (main course) and rum-n-raspberry ice cream (dessert) will not be savoured by most astronauts. For one thing, the heart of the galaxy is a very long way off. And for another, most people don't have a very good sense of smell or taste while in space.

"Two things are infinite: the Universe and human stupidity; and I'm not sure about the Universe."

Albert Einstein (1879–1955)
German theoretical physicist

IS THE UNIVERSE GETTING BIGGER?

By looking at the way stuff moves in space – you know, star systems and galaxies and so on – we can try to work out whether the Universe is still expanding from the original 'Big Bang'.

We think there was a beginning to the Universe, and we know that its galaxies are moving further apart into a seemingly 'endless', infinite space... So now we've been trying to work out if this expansion is getting faster, or slowing down. In other words, it seems that the Universe has been getting bigger and bigger for a very long time – so when is it finally going to stop?!

The latest news is rather exciting.

Astronomers say: the expansion of the Universe *is* getting faster and faster. That means the space between the galaxies is getting even bigger.

If this *accelerating* expansion goes on, over millions of years, all the galaxies beyond our own local group will be so far away that it will be hard to detect them. It will seem as though, one by one, the lights in the sky are going out.

In that case, the future of the Universe is not necessarily bright. It could well be quite dark.

Spooky.

2

GOODNESS GRACIOUS, GREAT BALLS OF GAS!

It's time to rub shoulders with the true celebrities of the cosmos. Let's meet... THE STARS!

Brown dwarfs, red giants, white dwarfs, blue supergiants, black holes, yellow dwarfs, super-dense neutron stars... They're a colourful bunch, eh? There are billions upon billions of them out there and just like people, they are all individuals, with different types of personality. Stars are like A-list actors in Hollywood: they can be a bit difficult at times, but there would be very little action without them.

HOW CAN THE SUN

Normally, the Sun is too bright to look at, let alone try and judge its size. But picture yourself on a crisp, foggy morning. There's little to see in the sky, but you can just make out a big ball of dim light. This is our Sun. You marvel at how huge it is.

That faint ball of light is 150 million kilometres away. Let's say you have a flying car, and let's say you whizz off towards the Sun at 150 kilometres per hour. (And don't worry, there are no speeding laws in space except this one: nothing travels faster than the speed of light – or so we think!) The Sun is so far away that even at 150 kilometres per hour it would take you a million hours to get there (that's 114 years).

Even though the Sun is ages away, it still looks huge to us from planet Earth. That's because it's 1.5 million kilometres across! That's large enough to fit 109 Earths across its middle and well over a million Earths inside it.

BE A DWARF?

Just to go round the Sun once – assuming you could stand the heat, and that your car was up to it – you would have to fly at supersonic speed, non-stop, for 227 days.

Okay, you get the picture. The Sun is **BIG**. But compared to some stars, it really is a bit titchy. In fact, in the words of modern astronomers, it's a 'dwarf star'.

Let's take just one example. In the constellation of Orion is a supergiant by the name of Betelgeuse. If you could pick up Betelgeuse and plop it where the Sun is, at the centre of our solar system, it would swallow up the orbits of the four innermost planets – Mercury, Venus, Earth and Mars. The greedy thing!

WHAT MAKES SUNSHINE?

The Sun is the key to life on Earth. Without it there would be no light, no heat, no food to eat, no weather, no days, no seasons, no Earth as we know it. In fact, no Solar System at all, as the Sun drives everything that happens here.

And the Sun does all this by sheer power. It is a ball of fiery energy, which burns about 4 million tonnes of gas a second. That's as much energy as 7 trillion nuclear explosions every second. No wonder it's so flipping hot!

Because the centre of the Sun has a temperature of about 16 million degrees centigrade, it's hot enough to turn hydrogen into helium. So one of the Sun's main jobs is making new atoms. It is an atom-making machine that lights up the entire Solar System with sunshine power.

Science boffins believe the Sun has been doing this job for about 4.57 billion years. In all that time it has been a constant energy-giving star, sending out massive amounts of light from Solar System Central.

And it's not just in our solar system that sun power is crucial. Stars power our entire Universe. *Let there be light!*

DO STARS MAKE NOISE?

Ancient Greek thinker Pythagoras thought that the Sun, Moon and planets made music as they moved through space, though he *didn't* think it was something you could actually *hear*. And medieval maths boffin Johannes Kepler was certain that the planets were spaced out from the Sun in gaps that had something to do with musical scales.

But this 'music of the spheres' is not just mystical nonsense. Oh no. Today's astronomers take great interest in the different sounds that stars make.

When they 'listen in' they hear a regular, repeating pattern. This tells them that a star is pulsating, throbbing in space. The different sounds give astronomers information about the star's inner workings, its age, size, and the stuff that's in it.

Of course, the boffins cannot listen to stars *directly*. They have to convert the 'seismic waves' (vibrations) from stars into a form that humans can hear on Earth. It's a bit like being a 'space doctor' – placing a big stethoscope on a star and giving it a health check!

DO STARS LIVE FOREVER?

Stars need fuel to keep going, so they spend their lives desperately seeking stuff to burn.

For most of their lives these Sun-like stars burn hydrogen, turning it into helium. When stars *run out* of hydrogen, the boffins think that they just switch to helium and burn that instead. In fact, stars can burn carbon, neon, oxygen and silicon, too.

When a star uses up one type of fuel and changes to another, it sends out a warning: it swells up massively in size to become a *red giant*.

In the distant future our Sun is expected to become a red giant, expanding to 200 times its normal size. When that happens, the boffins expect it to swallow up the inner planets of the Solar System, including our beloved Earth!

But don't worry. It seems that Mars will survive, so we'll just have to move home and become Martians.

DO STARS EXPLODE?

And then some! An exploding star is called a supernova and it is extremely powerful. A supernova can release more energy in one minute than is released by all the normal stars in the entire Universe during that very same minute.

Star explosions like this happen to very big stars. When they run out of fuel to burn, these big guys blow up.

The burst of light they give out as they go supernova can be as much as our Sun emits over its entire lifetime. So it's easy to see how a supernova can often outshine the entire galaxy in which it sits.

Space boffins think that there is a supernova – in a galaxy the size of ours – every 50 years or so. So it's truly a very special firework display for stargazers!

WHY DO SUPERSTARS LIVE FAST AND DIE YOUNG?

Stars come in many sizes and many masses. Mass is a measure of the amount of stuff something contains. The mass of a star tells you how much gas is in it.

The smallest stars have about 100 times more mass than Jupiter. (This means that if Jupiter had been 100 times more massive, it would have been a star, not a planet.) The biggest stars are thought to have a mass about 100 times greater than the Sun's. These fellas are real monsters, but they don't last long.

The bigger the star, the shorter its life.

Monster stars have lifetimes that last in millions, not billions, of years. That's because they have a ravenous appetite and burn up gas like there's no tomorrow. And they have a habit of exploding.

But it's the little guys that count. These little chaps are about as massive as the Sun, or have less mass. There are far more tiddlers than there are monsters, and they have 'forever lifetimes'. A star with half as much mass as our Sun will go on burning for many billions of years.

IS ANYWHERE COMPLETELY DARK?

Sometimes, a star gets so amazingly massive that it cannot stop collapsing in on itself under the pressure of all that mass! This may happen because the star has too little fuel left, or because it is picking up a lot of extra stuff from somewhere close to it in space.

Having huge mass means exerting a lot of gravitational pull on surrounding things. So it could be that a massive star's gravity is attracting everything near it – including light – and stopping everything from escaping its massive pulling power.

They appear black, these massive stars, so the boffins like to call them black holes.

Aren't boffins clever with words?

Black holes could well be the darkest places anywhere in space. The trouble is, these things are so *perfectly* black that it's hard to actually find them.

DO BLACK HOLES TURN YOU INTO SPAGHETTI?

Our feet stay on the ground because Earth has a lot of mass, which has a gravitational pull on us (who have less mass). The closer you are to a massive object, the more its gravity is exerted upon you.

Now, black holes are meant to have LOOOOAAAADDDDSSSSS of mass. So much mass, in fact, that the difference in gravity exerted upon your head and upon your toes would be huge! This would have the effect of stretching your body into long, thin shapes – rather like spaghetti.

The name that the boffins give to this stretching effect is *spaghettification*. (I told you boffins were clever with their words.)

The spaghettification stretching power is so immense around a black hole that resistance is futile (useless!). But don't worry too much just yet. It's unlikely that anyone will be taking a peek into a black hole in the near future...

WHAT'S AT THE CENTRE OF THE MILKY WAY?

I'm sure you are now worrying about being turned into spaghetti. Worry not. Astronomers have found good evidence of black holes existing, but not in planet Earth's backyard! However, one of the key candidates is right at the middle of our own Milky Way Galaxy.

Don't panic! That's about 26,000 light years away, so it's hardly likely to swallow up the Earth next Wednesday.

There's a lot of matter – or mass – at the centre of the Milky Way, and in quite a small amount of space. It's exactly the kind of conditions where a black hole would thrive. So much so that the boffins think there is an enormous, *supermassive* black hole lurking there.

In fact, they think there may be supermassive black holes at the centre of most galaxies.

WHEN STARS DIE, WHAT HAPPENS TO ALL THEIR STUFF?

Listen: stars never really die. Many just slowly change into a different kind of star, and some explode to leave behind a ghostly relic of themselves. It all depends on their size, how much matter they have.

Remember: the smaller the star, the longer its life.

Small stars live for billions and billions of years. And when these little fellas do eventually run out of fuel, they keep on shining for a long time afterwards. When small stars get to this stage in their lives they're known as *white dwarfs*. Astronomers think that more than 97 per cent of the stars in our galaxy will end up like this.

The monster stars are rare, and they have a different story to tell.

The mid-sized ones become *red giants*, swelling up in size and changing colour as they go.

Big stars go bang, in a supernova, and then they become either black holes or *neutron stars*. Neutron stars are amazingly dense – as dense as the entire human population of the Earth squeezed down into the size of a sugar cube.

Now isn't that *sweet*?

So there are different life journeys a star can take. Each journey has an endpoint, and those endpoints are the white dwarfs, red giants, neutron stars, or black holes. Whichever way they go, stars are always blasting stuff out into space, stuff richly made of the chemical elements created inside the stars.

That leftover 'star stuff' is then part of the universal mixture – part of the recipe for a new generation of stars to be made out of the old.

It's the ultimate in recycling!

WHAT'S THE DIFFERENCE BETWEEN ME, A PLANET, AND A STAR?

You are made of star stuff. Sounds mad, but it's absolutely true.

The carbon in your skin, the iron in your blood, the calcium in your teeth – these elements are just some of the stuff cooked up inside stars and then ejected into space to make new stars, planets, and other things such as people.

Take carbon. It's an element on Earth that's important to all life. Carbon is made in stars of all sizes, but it is not burned up by them. It survives the starry furnaces and is released, along with other elements, as the star itself goes through a sort of recycling process towards the end of its life. It is then free to make up parts of other stuff – like us!

Astronomers can tell what's inside stars by reading the starlight that eventually falls to Earth. These experts used to think that there was a big difference between stars and planets. But these days we think of them as one great big family of stuff.

At the beginning of our own solar system, everything formed at the same time from a collapsing gas cloud. The four small, *inner* planets – Mercury, Venus, Earth and Mars – are mostly made of rock and metal. But the four *outer* planets – Jupiter, Saturn, Uranus and Neptune – are largely composed of hydrogen and helium gas, just like the Sun itself.

So what makes a star so different?

Stars shine and planets don't – that's the main difference. There are planets and stars of various sizes, masses and fillings. But the big distinction between a large planet such as Jupiter and a star such as the Sun is that Jupiter *just isn't quite massive enough* to get the hydrogen gas burning at the very heart of itself.

BRAIN BURN!

Human beings are the product of a grand and cosmic recycling scheme in space. *Groovy!*

WHAT IS LIGHT?

Light is travelling energy.

When you dive-bomb into a swimming pool (probably not allowed by the lifeguard) the energy created by your body hitting the water can be seen in all the waves moving across the water. The important thing is that the water wave is not made up of water. The wave is made up of energy. And it is the *wave* that does the moving, not the water itself.

Light is also energy that travels in waves, although it can travel through space as well as through a substance such as water.

You can think of light as 'packets' of energy, called photons, which our eyes are able to see. There are loads of different ways to produce photons of light. In space, the photons that travel to us as starlight are created at the very centre of stars – such as our Sun – that burn up hydrogen gas.

HOW QUICK IS LIGHT?

It's the quickest thing in the Universe! Well, as far as we know, nothing can go faster, but the boffins are always trying to find out.

Light moves at a speed of about 300,000 kilometres every second. Because we know this, the speed of light is a useful way of measuring big distances in space.

Light is so swift it can go around the Earth's equator ten times every second. It can then nip over to the Moon from Earth in a second, or cruise to the Sun in eight minutes.

It could be a very nifty way to travel, if only you could jump on a light beam.

(Please don't try this).

But distances in space are so vast that even light takes more than four years to get to the next star (after our local one). And light would need about 100,000 years to get across our Milky Way, which gives you a pretty good idea of just how enormous our galaxy is.

IS WHAT I'M SEEING ACTUALLY THERE?

We can see things in space, either because they are *emitting* (giving off) light or because they are *reflecting* it. We know that this emitted or reflected light is often travelling vast distances to get to us, and that this journey might take a very long time.

So... some of the things you see in the night sky may no longer be there!

Imagine a star went bang somewhere in our galaxy in a really bright, supernova explosion.

And imagine that it was so far away that it took light from that star about 100,000 years to reach Earth. Even though the supernova was brilliantly bright, we wouldn't actually see the explosion on Earth for 100,000 years *AFTER* it took place.

In all that time, in between the explosion and us seeing it, we would be gazing up and looking at a star that was not actually there anymore. Spooky!

3
TIME, TIME, AND TIME AGAIN

I suppose it must be time to talk about... TIME!

We all think, rather smugly, that we've got a good handle on time. As human beings, we've decided how to 'measure' time. We 'read' and 'tell' the time, all the time. But where did time *come from* in the first place?

It doesn't take much to confuse us once we really start to investigate it. What if time sped up, or slowed down, or decided to go backwards? What if there were holes or gaps in time? Then we really would be all over the place.

HOW DID WE PUT TIME TOGETHER?

Okay, so you can't exactly 'build' time. But we measure time in a way that suits our experience on the planet: the time it takes for Earth to rotate around its axis once is what we call a 'day' (24 hours). The time it takes for Earth to travel around the Sun once is a 'year' (365 days).

But the bigger *story* of time has been harder to piece together.

When the Industrial Revolution came along (in the late 18th century) and we started digging in the ground to look for fuels, engineers discovered the fossilized remains of many animals in the rocks. Animals such as the dinosaurs, which no longer live on Earth.

Our story of Earth's origin suddenly started to change. The remains of these extinct beasties were found in crazy places – sea creatures on hilltops, polar bears at the Equator, and elephants on the Moon (okay, so I made the last one up). Planet Earth must have gone through big changes, both to its rocks and to this host of bizarre beasts, to explain all the things that were being discovered.

So, instead of thinking that the Earth and the Universe formed around 6,000 years ago, people started to realize it must have taken millions upon millions of years for all of Earth's changes to happen.

HOW DO WE KNOW THE AGE OF THINGS IN SPACE?

So, the boffins realized it had taken millions of years for the changes in the rocks and the animals to take place, and this led to huge changes in the way we thought about time. People began to understand that the whole Universe around us was incredibly, amazingly old.

The boffins worked out how to date the rocks on Earth by measuring how long it takes stuff in the rocks to waste away. This helped us to discover that our little planet is truly ancient, at an age of 4.5 billion years. That's 4,500 million years old.

In the 1960s and '70s, Apollo astronauts visited the Moon and brought back rocks. These turned out to be the same age as rocks on Earth. This was also true for meteorites, and for bits of Mars that had fallen to Earth. So they must have been created at the same time.

Astronomers are also estimating the age of the Sun using computer models. They think it's even more ancient than the Earth, at about 4.57 billion years of age. And this makes good sense. After all, you can't have a Solar System without the Sun setting up home there first!

IF A WARDROBE HAS 3 DIMENSIONS, WHAT IS THE 4TH?

Your wardrobe is an object with three dimensions, which describe the space it is occupying – its height, its depth and its width. But your world also has a *fourth* dimension. The first three dimensions are space. The fourth is *time*.

Let's think about that wardrobe again...

You probably think you know exactly where your wardrobe is going to be a week next Wednesday. But, even though you don't notice it, your wardrobe is constantly moving. Sure, it's always in that dusty corner of your bedroom. It doesn't shift in terms of space. But that's only *three* of the four dimensions, isn't it?

In terms of time, it's a different story.

Take another look at your wardrobe. Is it moving? No? Are you *sure*? *Definitely* not moving? Actually, it is. It is moving in space-time. It's staying where it is in the three dimensions of space, but the *fourth* dimension of time is changing.

So – even though you are not seeing this happen, that fourth dimension is most definitely there.

DOES TIME ALWAYS GO AT THE SAME SPEED?

It's easy to get the impression that time always flows at the same rate because mostly it seems to, in day-to-day life. But, in fact, there is no such thing as *THE* time, a flow of time that is the same throughout the Universe.

Remember Einstein? (Yes, the guy with the wild and wacky white hair who rewrote the rules of science...) Well, he showed us that our day-to-day understanding of time is wrong. Time is not 'absolute'. It is 'relative'. This means that the rate at which time flows depends upon where you are and how fast you are travelling.

For one thing, moving clocks run more slowly than stationary ones. This is true – even if you use the most accurate clocks in the world, known as atomic clocks.

Imagine you have two of these 'atomic' clocks. You pop one on board a spaceship, and the other stays at home on Earth. And imagine the spaceship whizzes off to a nearby star system, at half the speed of light.

When the spaceship returns, the atomic clock on Earth says 30 years have gone by. But the clock on board the spaceship says the total journey time was only 26 years.

It seems incredible, but only because we assume that the two clocks tick at the same rate. But they do not!

"Even a stopped clock gives the right time twice a day."
from the film *Withnail And I* (1986)

HOW IS MY BODY LIKE A CLOCK?

BRAIN BURN!
If time goes more slowly on Jupiter, does this mean life there would be less stressful?

Strangely, people don't always age at the same rate. It's not just mechanical and atomic clocks that are affected by speed. It's *biological* clocks, too, such as the ageing of your own body.

Here is a story of twin brothers...

Just after celebrating their 21st birthday together, one of the twins (an astronaut) goes on a long trip into space, travelling at 96 per cent of the speed of light.

It makes sense that if the astronaut is away for 14 Earth years, he will be 35 years old on his return to Earth. As the astronaut descends the stairs of the spaceship, he naturally assumes that his twin brother is also 35. So, as you can imagine, he is pretty horrified to discover that his brother is actually 71 years old.

This puzzle is a real-life effect of travelling in time, and is known as the Twin Paradox.

Although we have never tested this effect using real people, we know it to be true. The facts have been checked using atomic clocks, flown in aeroplanes travelling at different speeds around the Earth.

IS TIME THE SAME ON BIGGER PLANETS?

Time is not even the same on different planets…

Take our little planet, for example. Time on Earth passes at different rates in different places. And all this weird time business partly depends on the strength of gravity in these different locations.

Imagine yourself in two different places on planet Earth: a sunny beach and on top of Mount Everest.

The sunny beach will be closer to the heart of the planet, and that means the pull of gravity (towards the centre of the Earth) will be greater in this location. Because of this, clocks will run *slightly* more slowly here. On top of Mount Everest the pull of gravity is weaker, which means clocks will run a little faster.

Once again, the facts have been checked by those egg-headed boffins using highly accurate atomic clocks. The clocks that were sent up to high altitudes, where there is less gravity, showed marginally faster times than the clocks on much lower ground.

Gravity is stronger on more massive planets, which means that clocks would run more slowly there. So it is true. Time itself would be slower.

Blimey.

HOW DO YOU BUILD A TIME MACHINE?

If there's one thing in this great big Universe that you cannot mess with, it's time. Science fiction writer H G Wells knew this only too well. So he went and messed with it. In 1895, he wrote an amazing novel about time travel called *The Time Machine*.

After all, if you can move freely in space, why not also in time?

Imagine you have your own time machine, delivered brand-new to your door. Where first? The last days of the Roman Empire? The Middle Ages? Or to the very end of the Universe itself? The Middle Ages. Good choice.

Okay, let's look at the instructions carefully… Temporal camshaft. *Check*. Fourth-dimensional perambulator. *Check*. Ignition. *Check*. Ignition?! Hang on a minute. Exactly how are these time machines meant to work?!

If you want to build a time machine to travel into the future, you need a spacecraft that can move pretty close to the speed of light. As the spacecraft approaches this speed, time moves more slowly. Once you get back to Earth, you will hardly have aged. But decades, or even *centuries*, will have passed 'back home'.

Bingo! You've arrived in the future.

Travelling backwards in time is even trickier! To do that you would need the kind of machine that works using the mind-warping, time-tickling technology of wormholes…

ARE THERE HOLES IN SPACE-TIME?

One of the 'least impossible' ways to travel in time could be the wormhole, a theoretical region of space-time that is *warped*. It is a potential 'short cut' in space and time through which we might be able to travel. The boffins think that wormholes might exist, but they have no evidence of them just yet.

But there may be snags. Imagine you create a wormhole. And imagine you're just busting to journey back in time to dote on a *Diplodocus*. Set the dial for the Jurassic!

But hang on. You would not be able to travel back in time to a date *before* the wormhole was actually created. This may explain why we've never been overrun by tourists from the future. We've not had the technology to create a wormhole. Not yet.

Unlike a black hole, which is a one-way journey to nowhere, a wormhole has two mouths – an entrance and an exit – and they are joined by a single 'throat' or tunnel. Stuff may 'travel' from one mouth to the other by passing through the throat. We haven't observed a wormhole yet, but the Universe is still young. And we haven't been looking for very long.

If the boffins can just find a way of keeping a wormhole throat open, some think it could be turned into a cosmic time machine. **Wow.**

The amazing
TIME-O-MATIC
Making your time-travel dreams a reality!

4

THE GREAT BIG FUTURISTIC SPACE ADVENTURE

Coming to a cinema near you soon... THE FUTURE!

We experience the future all the time – or, at least, our idea of what it might be like – through books, films, television, and so on. Why are we so obsessed with it?

It's the outward urge! Space is a vast, *vast* expanse, and as human beings we can't wait to discover what lies beyond our known limits. We see our future 'out there'. We are *itching* to get out into space, make it our own, and find out all we can about it.

But how will this change our relationship with the Universe? Will it make us any more a part of it? Or will it make us feel even more alone than we were before?

WHERE DID SCIENCE FICTION BEGIN?

Listen: humans haven't always been fascinated by the future. We haven't always had an urge to sail out into space, the final frontier. But we have been curious about the cosmos for a very long time. You *could* say, in fact, that science fiction writing began with early mythological stories, or with the early theories of the ancient Greeks.

Much later, in the early 1600s, came the invention of the telescope. Italian astronomer Galileo was pretty handy with this exciting new instrument. He discovered four giant moons around Jupiter, and that our Milky Way was made up of thousands of stars. And when Galileo spied the Moon, he saw mountains and craters not unlike those down here! When Galileo wrote about his discoveries in 1610, he urged his readers to imagine...

What would it be like to walk on the Moon?

Galileo's awesome discoveries inspired writers to imagine what life might be like in space, what it might be like on another planet. And so science fiction truly began in the way that we know it now. The first 'sci-fi' stories were about space travel. They imagined sailing out into space, and the first destination was (yes, you've guessed it): the Moon.

BRAIN BURN!

What if science fiction writers really did have the power to 'write' the future?

WHO INVENTED SPACE TRAVEL?

Some time between 1620 and 1630, astronomer Johannes Kepler wrote a story called *Somnium*. Kepler was probably the most important astronomer in the world at the time. He was a bright fellow. He believed space travel would be possible one day. And he knew we'd have to beat Earth's gravity to get to places such as the Moon. In Kepler's tale, lunar demons travel between Earth and the Moon on a 'bridge of darkness'. It sounds fantastic! But here's the crafty bit: the bridge carries travellers out into space, to a point of 'special gravity' where they can just drift down to the Moon's surface. If only it were that simple in real life!

Another early sci-fi story was *The Man in the Moon*, written by a Welsh bishop, Francis Godwin, and published in 1638. Bishop Godwin also understood that the first problem of space travel was gravity. In his tale, a traveller uses a flock of geese to travel to China. But instead, he accidentally ends up on the Moon.

In 1660, the world's first science organization – the Royal Society – was founded in England. Its members decided that a space voyage to another world was, in fact, a very real possibility. And the rest... is history!

WAS NEIL ARMSTRONG A MODERN EXPLORER?

It's a story of exploration.

Long before the invention of the telescope, the world was a place of travel and trade. As maps became more accurate, ships stopped creeping along coastlines and started taking off across the seas. Vikings settled in America, and Christopher Columbus (1451–1506) rediscovered it about 500 years later. This was like finding another 'world' on Earth, just as Galileo went on to find other worlds in space.

Galileo's telescope was a kind of ship. It took him, and all the other onlookers on Earth, to places in space nobody had ever imagined. The telescope brought the Moon to life and made it *real* in our minds. It became a reachable place – another *world*, close to our own.

We began to think about the possibilities: are there aliens on the Moon? What would it be like to walk over that craggy landscape?

The long journey to Neil Armstrong's 'one small step' on the Moon, in 1969, began with Galileo and the telescope in 1609.

WHO OWNS SPACE?

Yaargh! Let's hark back to the days of pirates on the high seas. When they raided ships, they wouldn't search for gold, silver or pieces of eight. *Oh no.* They would head straight for the hold – where the ship's maps and clocks were kept. The most valuable cargoes were the tools of science, the tools of *discovery*.

So why is science so valuable?

Navigation and seafaring have always been important for trade. If you can discover something, and sell it to the rest of the human race, you can make a lot of money.

Spacefaring may also bring fame, fortune and bounty!

Earth's natural resources are beginning to dwindle, so it's no wonder that its nations dream of sailing out to distant worlds – to plant a flag on them and say, 'Okay, that's ours now!' Owning a moon or an asteroid, where there are lots of natural fuels and materials, could be worth an absolute *fortune*.

But it's worth remembering that space travel is an expensive business. A big investment. You'd have to put in a lot of money to plant your flag on another planet, say. And there's no guarantee you'll get anything back.

And just because you've landed on another object in space, does that really mean you can call it your own? Surely that's rather cheeky!

After all... who owns planet Earth? Maybe it's aliens, and we're all working for *them*.

ARE THERE ALIENS IN OUR SOLAR SYSTEM?

Today's space missions to Mars look for water, among other things. For where there is water, there might be life. Like Earth, Mars has water ice caps at its poles and some scientists think there is liquid water below the southern ice cap.

Another possible home for alien life is Europa, one of Jupiter's biggest moons. Europa is smooth, completely covered by an icy crust. *Underneath* that ice, the giant moon may be hiding a vast underground ocean – and tiny microbes, similar to those in Earth's oceans, may be lurking in those subterranean seas.

ARE THERE OTHER EARTHS?

In 1543, a very important book was published, written by a Polish astronomer called Nicholas Copernicus. This book suggested that the Sun, not the Earth, was at the centre of our small solar system. Before Copernicus, people did not think that the Earth was a planet. They thought it was...

(BIG FANFARE): THE CENTRE OF EVERYTHING IN THE UNIVERSE

Ever since Copernicus, astronomers have been wondering about other planets like ours. Since the 19th century we've known that most stars in the sky are like our Sun, and that many of them have planets in orbit around them. Such planets are called 'extrasolar' planets. It was only in the 1990s that we found the first official example. But today, we know of more than 5,000.

This includes several Earth-like planets such as Kepler-452b, which takes 385 Earth days to orbit around its star, a bit longer than one Earth year, and it is the right distance from its star that liquid water could exist at the planet's surface. However, we've not yet found a planet that is exactly like Earth... yet.

DO ALIENS LOOK LIKE ME?

Here's the thing: if Earth's not the only planet out there, and there are life forms on other planets, then Earth's not so special after all. It's just another place where life is possible.

And here's another thing: biologists such as Charles Darwin started thinking about how creatures on Earth change over time – how they evolve. But his ideas on evolution don't just work for creatures on Earth. They work for aliens, too. Creatures on other planets would also need to change and evolve to suit the environment in which they live.

Since the vast majority of extrasolar planets are nothing like Earth, it makes sense that aliens wouldn't look like humans. It would be very spooky indeed if there were another 'you' out there in space!

IF SPACE IS FULL OF ALIENS, HOW COME THEY HAVEN'T VISITED US YET?

This question is known as Fermi's Paradox, as it was posed by the Italian physicist Enrico Fermi.

And it's a very good point. If intelligent life is out there, why hasn't it made contact with us yet?

Firstly, space is mind-bogglingly big. Intelligent aliens have probably noticed this whenever they've thought of popping down to Earth for a take-away meal. Maybe space travel ain't that easy. Blimey, we've only managed to visit the Moon in the last 50 years of so-called 'space exploration', and that's only one light second away!

Secondly, perhaps they are watching and waiting. Waiting until we evolve a bit more, get a bit more clever. Once we've evolved, maybe they'll come and invite us over for tea, to join in with their intergalactic chit-chat and exchange wild tales of Universal exploration.

Thirdly, maybe all the smart aliens have never bothered with technology and travel. Maybe they are happy just plodding around their planet, gathering and hunting, like hunter-gatherers are meant to do.

And finally...

Maybe we *are* being visited. All the time. That's why people have spotted UFOs, flying saucers, and believe they have already enjoyed that steaming cup of tea (and maybe even a biscuit) up on the aliens' Mother Ship.

WOULD ALIENS WANT TO STEAL OUR STUFF?

Isn't it funny, the way we always imagine aliens to be super-intelligent?

Okay, fair enough. If they've jetted across the furthest reaches of space for a hot dog, and we can only manage the poxy Moon, maybe they ARE smarter than us. But if that's true, what would they want with Earth stuff? Imagine an alien fumbling with a toaster, filing its nails with your skateboard, or trying to work out why you only have two shoes.

Ah, but maybe they've run out of resources. Like us, perhaps they have a growing population that they find hard to feed and water. But if they're THAT advanced they're hardly going to jet halfway across the galaxy looking for wood. They would probably look for raw materials in their own solar system, closer to home.

BRAIN BURN!

What if aliens have already visited Earth, way back in the distant past?

GLOSSARY

Words in **bold** refer to other glossary entries.

ARMSTRONG, NEIL (Born 1930)
An American astronaut who was the first person to set foot on the Moon, in July 1969, one of only 12 human beings ever to do so. Armstrong was the Commander of the Apollo 11 mission to land two men on the Moon.

ATOM
A basic unit of matter. The word atom comes from the Greek word *atomos*, which means 'uncuttable'.

ATOMIC CLOCK
An extremely accurate clock, which works by using the natural behaviour of atoms as its time-keeping element.

AXIS
An imaginary line around which a three-dimensional object, such as a planet, rotates. Earth's axis is the imaginary line that runs through the inside of the planet, from the North Pole to the South Pole.

BETELGEUSE
A red **supergiant** star in the **constellation** of Orion. Betelgeuse is the ninth-brightest star in the night sky.

BIG BANG
A theory of the beginning and evolution of the **Universe**, which is supported by current observations. The theory says that the **Universe** began about 13.75 **billion** years ago, and continues to expand to this day.

BILLION
One thousand **million** (or 1,000,000,000).

BIOLOGICAL CLOCK
A roughly 24-hour cycle in the natural behaviour of living things, including plants and animals.

BLACK HOLE
A region of space from which nothing, including light, can escape. **Boffins** think that black holes are made by very, very dense matter causing a massive warping of space-time.

BOFFIN
A familiar term used to describe scientists, engineers, and other particularly clever people. In short, a geezer (or geezeress) who knows lots of important stuff.

COLUMBUS, CHRISTOPHER
(1451–1506) An Italian navigator and explorer whose voyages across the Atlantic Ocean made Europeans aware of North and South America.

CONSTELLATION
An area of the night sky used to refer to a pattern of prominent stars, which appear to be close to one another.

COPERNICUS, NICHOLAS
(1473–1543) A Polish astronomer who was the first in modern times to suggest a Sun-centred solar system, moving the Earth from the centre of the **Universe**.

COSMOS
From a Greek word, *kosmos*, which means 'order' or 'harmony' – the opposite of chaos. It is still used as another word for space or **Universe**.

DARK ENERGY A supposed form of energy that is spread through all of space and which tends to increase the rate the **Universe** is expanding.

DARK MATTER An invisible form of matter that is thought to make up the vast majority of **mass** in the **Universe**. Though it cannot be seen, the existence of dark matter can be guessed at by the behaviour of visible matter, or 'light' matter.

DARWIN, CHARLES (1809–82) An English naturalist who is credited with realizing that all species of life on Earth have descended over time from common ancestors.

EINSTEIN, ALBERT (1879–1955) A German scientist who is regarded as one of the most influential **boffins** of all time. His thoughts on space and time were included in his Special and General theories of relativity.

FERMI, ENRICO (1901–54) An Italian scientist. Fermi is mainly remembered for his work on the idea of using nuclear energy for the generation of electrical power.

GALAXY A massive collection of stars, gas and dust bound together by **gravity** in one system. Galaxies range from dwarfs, with as few as ten **million** stars, up to giants with one **trillion** stars. The galaxy in which our local star, the Sun, sits is called the **Milky Way Galaxy**.

GALILEO GALILEI (1564–1642) An Italian astronomer and philosopher who played a major role in the early development of modern science. Galileo was the first to discover the four largest moons of Jupiter, named 'the Galilean moons' in his honour.

GODWIN, FRANCIS (BISHOP) (1562–1633) Bishop of Llandaff in Wales and author of perhaps the first alien contact story in the English language. Godwin's tale, *The Man in the Moon* (published in 1638), also supported the ideas of **Copernicus** and used an early idea of **gravity** in the story's description of travelling to the Moon.

GRAVITY A natural phenomenon by which bodies with **mass** attract one another. Gravity is responsible for keeping the Earth in **orbit** around the Sun, and the Moon in **orbit** around the Earth. The effects of the Moon and Sun's gravity are also responsible for the tides of the ocean on Earth.

INDUSTRIAL REVOLUTION A period of time, mostly during the 1700s and 1800s, when major changes in producing goods and foods had a drastic effect on living conditions in the UK. Later, this major turning point in human history spread throughout Europe, the United States, and the rest of the world.

INFINITE This word describes something that appears to have no limits in size, extent, time or space.

KEPLER, JOHANNES (1571–1630)
German astronomer and mathematician, best known for working out the laws that describe the motion of the planets around the Sun. Kepler also wrote one of the first ever science fiction stories, called *Somnium*.

MASS
The mass of a body is a measure of the amount of matter ('stuff') it contains. Weight results from the action of **gravity** on the mass of a body.

MILKY WAY GALAXY
The Milky Way, or simply the Galaxy, is the **galaxy** in which our **solar system** is located. It is one of **billions** of galaxies in the **Universe**.

MILLION
A thousand thousand (or 1,000,000).

NASA
Stands for the National Aeronautics and Space Administration. It is an agency of the United States government and is responsible for America's missions into space, such as the Apollo missions to the Moon and those of the Space Shuttle in Earth's orbit.

NEUTRON STAR
A type of star that has collapsed under its own **gravity** so that it is almost entirely composed of neutrons (particles with no electrical charge). The density of a typical neutron star is equivalent to the entire human population being squeezed down into the size of a sugar cube.

NUCLEAR EXPLOSION
An explosion from a nuclear weapon that gets its destructive force from the nuclei (central cores) of **atoms**. Nuclear processes are so powerful that even small nuclear weapons can devastate an entire city.

ORBIT
The curved path of one body around another, such as the orbit of a planet around the Sun. The natural phenomenon that keeps bodies in orbit is **gravity**.

PHOTON
The basic unit of light. A photon is an elementary particle, and has no **mass**.

PYTHAGORAS (c. 570–c. 495 BCE)
Pythagoras was a mathematician and philosopher who lived in ancient Greece. He and his followers believed that everything was related to mathematics, and that numbers were the key to the **Universe**.

RED GIANT
A bright and large star of medium **mass**, which is in the late stage of its evolution.

RED SHIFT SURVEY
Astronomers can observe 'red-shifted' light from galaxies that are moving away from us. They use it to measure vast distances and create red shift surveys – vast 'maps' of the sky, intended to plot the positions of galaxies and to discover the large-scale structure of the **Universe**.

SOLAR SYSTEM The Sun and all the other bodies bound to it by **gravity**, including: the four small inner planets – Mercury, Venus, Earth and Mars – which are mostly made of rock and metal; the four outer planets – Jupiter, Saturn, Uranus and Neptune – which are mostly made of hydrogen and helium; and all the minor bodies, such as asteroids, comets, and dwarf planets such as Pluto.

SPEED OF LIGHT The speed of light is 299,792,458 metres per second, or roughly 300,000 kilometres per second. Light could travel between the Sun and the Earth approximately 173 times in one day.

SUPERGIANT The most massive of stars. Supergiants come in all colours of the spectrum, from young, blue supergiants to older, red supergiants such as **Betelgeuse**.

SUPERNOVA The intensely bright explosion of a star, which expels most of the star's material into surrounding space.

SUPERSONIC A word used to describe a speed that is greater than the speed of sound, which is 343 metres per second.

TRILLION A million million (or 1,000,000,000,000).

UNIVERSE The Universe consists of everything that exists, the whole of space and time, and all the matter and energy within it. Now and again, it is also referred to in this book as the **cosmos**.

WELLS, H G (1866–1946) An English writer, best known for his stories of science fiction. Along with French author Jules Verne, Wells has been called 'The Father of Science Fiction'.

WORMHOLE A theoretical feature of space-time. A wormhole is a 'short cut' through space and time, a tunnel that may allow a traveller a speedier journey between two points.

INDEX

aliens 7, 54, 55, 56, 57
ancient Greeks 50
Apollo mission 41, 58
Armstrong, Neil 52, 58
astronauts 20, 41
astronomers 10, 17, 18, 27, 35, 51, 54
atomic clocks 44, 45, 58
atoms 26, 58
axis 13, 41, 58

Betelgeuse 25, 58
Big Bang 9, 21, 58
biological clocks 44
black holes 30, 31, 33, 47, 58
brown dwarfs 23

calcium 35
carbon 11, 28, 35
Columbus, Christopher 52, 58
Copernicus, Nicholas 54, 58
cosmic web 17
creation stories 14–15

dark energy 18, 59
dark matter 18, 59
Darwin, Charles 55, 59
dinosaurs 41
distances 11, 16, 17, 37
dwarf stars 25

Einstein, Albert 19, 20, 43, 59
energy 26, 36
Europa 54
expansion 21

Fermi, Enrico 56, 59
Fermi's Paradox 56
fossils 41
fourth dimension 42

galaxies 10, 13, 16, 17, 18, 19, 21, 31, 59
Galileo 50, 52, 59
gas 26, 29
Godwin, Francis 51, 59
gravity 30, 31, 45, 51, 59

heat 26
helium 11, 26, 28, 35
hydrogen 11, 26, 28, 35, 36

Industrial Revolution 41, 59
iron 11, 35

Jupiter 29, 35, 50, 54

Kepler, Johannes 27, 51, 60
Kiowa Apaches 14

lifetimes (of stars) 28–29, 32
light 10, 11, 17, 18, 19, 26, 36–37
look-back time 11

maps 7, 17, 52, 53
Mars 25, 28, 35, 41, 54
mass 19, 29, 30, 31, 36, 60
matter 18, 31
Mercury 25, 35
Milky Way 13, 20, 31, 37, 50, 60
Moon 17, 27, 41, 51, 52

moons 18, 50, 54
music 27
mythology 14–15, 50

NASA 20, 60
navigation 13, 53
neon 28
Neptune 35
neutron stars 23, 33, 60
night sky 7, 13, 19
noise 27

Orion 25
oxygen 28

photons 36, 60
planets 13, 18, 27, 35, 54
Proxima Centauri 17
Pythagoras 27, 60

red giants 23, 28, 33, 60
red shift 10
red shift surveys 17, 60
Royal Society 51

Saturn 35
science fiction 46, 50, 51
seasons 13, 26
shape (of Universe) 19
silicon 28
smell (of space or Universe) 20
solar systems 16, 25, 26, 28, 35, 61
space-time 42, 47
space travel 20, 41, 51, 52, 53

spaghettification 31
speed of light 17, 24, 37, 46, 61
speed of time 43, 46
stargazing 11, 13
starlight 17, 18, 36
stories 14–15, 50, 51
Sun 13, 17, 19, 24–25, 26, 27, 28, 41
sunlight 19, 26
supergiants 23, 25, 61
supernovas 29, 33, 37, 61

taste (of space or Universe) 20
telescope 13, 50, 52
temperature 26
time 7, 11, 40–47
time travel 11, 44, 46
Twin Paradox 44

UFOs 56
Uranus 35

Venus 25, 35

Wells, H G 46, 61
West Africa 14
white dwarfs 23, 32
wormholes 47, 61

FURTHER READING

BOOKS

Space Hoppers – Mark Brake
FutureWorld – Mark Brake
Eyewitness: Time and Space – John Gribbin
A Wrinkle in Time – Madeleine L'Engle
Space, Black Holes and Stuff – Glenn Murphy
The Time and Space of Uncle Albert – Russell Stannard

WEBSITES

NASA's Space Place:
https://spaceplace.nasa.gov/

ESA (European Space Agency):
www.esa.int/esaKIDSen/

HOW TO THINK LIKE A BOFFIN

Here are five tips to help you think like a boffin. When you are trying to formulate a scientific theory:

1. If possible, try to get independent proof of the 'facts', as you see them.

2. Think about whether your theory can be shown to be false. In other words, is it 'testable'?

3. Try to test out your theory with observation and experiment. Do other boffins get the same results?

4. Spin more than one theory – don't simply run with the first idea that pops into your head.

5. Persuade other boffins to shoot down your theory in flames (in other words, strongly disagree with it). Debating theories, based on evidence and observation, is another key tip to thinking like a boffin.

And remember: there is nothing wrong with being a boffin. The Universe needs boffins.

Boffins are *brilliant*.